My thanks to the Media Centre at Catterick Garrison, Richmondshire District Council, the North Yorkshire Police and Andrew Baxter of the Forensic Science Service; particular thanks to Angela Dodd-Crompton and Adrian Taplin (Major, retired). They all did their best – any mistakes, and creative interpretations of reality, are entirely of my own making.

Dedicated to the people of Arkengarthdale, a hardy and independent folk, whom it has been my privilege to get to know.

Contents

Characters

Detective Inspector (DI) Charles Neville: a police officer
Detective Sergeant (DS) Helen Scott: a police officer
Fiona Russell: a crime analyst
Kay Harding: a police doctor
Jonathan Greene: a journalist
Alan Reid: an army major
Terry Reid: Alan's brother
Mrs Reid: Terry and Alan's mother

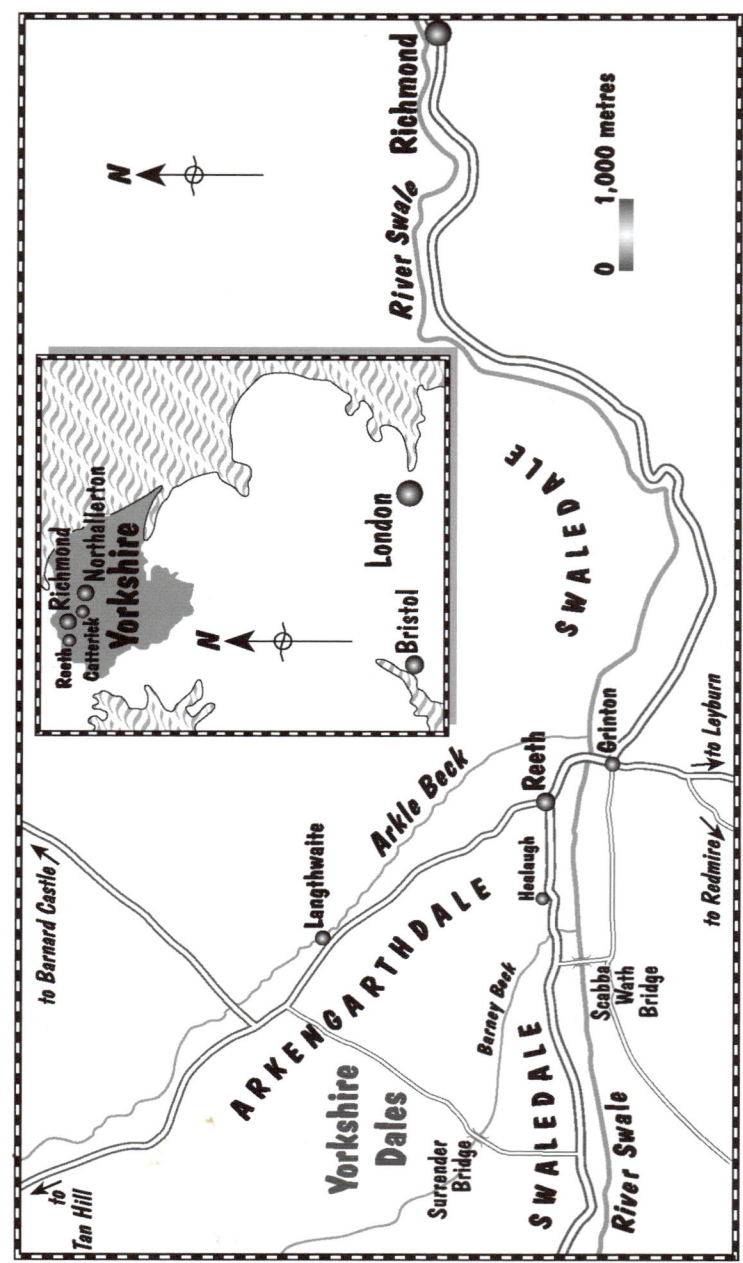

Chapter 1 *A moorland death*

The first killing went well. Perfectly, in fact. Though I always knew it would. I had planned it well. Arrangements, organisation – these are things I'm good at. Now I've discovered I'm good at killing too.

At six o'clock in the morning I turned the car left off the road towards Tan Hill. The highest pub in England is at Tan Hill. But there's just the pub there, nothing else – no houses, no other buildings. The nearest village is eight kilometres away, the nearest shop twelve kilometres. This is wild, treeless country. There would be amazing views later, when the sun got up, but I wasn't interested in them.

I continued along a dirt road across moorland, stopping only when the car could no longer be seen from the road. Not that there was ever much traffic here.

I got out and stretched, enjoying the sharp cold of the early autumn air. To make myself less noticeable against the dull green grasses of the countryside around me, I was wearing hiking clothes and boots of a similar greeny colour. I took an old brown backpack off the back seat of the car and checked inside. There was a map, a bottle of water, gloves, binoculars and some sandwiches. I took out the gloves and put them on. I also had a hand-held GPS – there were no paths where I was going. In more ways than one I was making my way into the unknown. It was a journey of discovery, one that I had promised myself for some time.

It took me two hours to walk across the wild moorland to where I wanted to be – two hours that seemed like no time at all. Excitement and nervousness were building up inside me in equal measure. In my mind I was going through the different possibilities of what might happen – yet I knew I would be successful.

Finally I arrived at the place I had chosen. There was an old, long-empty house beside a dirty-brown stream, which laughed its way down the side of the hill. The house was roofless and one wall was falling down. There were piles of old stones lying around. I found a stone that felt comfortable in my right hand, heavy and with sharp edges. Later I would use it.

A path turned this way and that up the hillside, past the house and over a wooden bridge across the stream. The path is well known to walkers, though not especially popular. The chances of a single walker taking advantage of this bright autumn morning were good, but there was unlikely to be a whole crowd of them. Then later, when the body was found, the police would think the killer had come along the same path as the walker, rather than over the pathless moorland. They would start searching in the wrong places. I had chosen well.

I took off my gloves, got my binoculars and a sandwich out of my backpack, and sat down on a large stone to wait. From where I was, I would be able see anyone coming from a long way away, but they would have difficulty seeing me.

I had hardly finished my sandwich when a man appeared in the distance, walking in my direction. Quickly I put on my gloves, picked up my chosen stone and hid behind the back wall of the house. I waited. My heart went faster. I took deep breaths to slow it down. I had a picture in my mind of the man coming nearer. My excitement rose; my nervousness disappeared. I heard the sound of footsteps on the dirt path. Coming near. Nearer. I raised my stone. This was the moment of truth.

And then it was done.

The man lay on his side on the ground by my feet. His longish grey hair had fallen over his face. His eyes were closed, but there was movement under the eyelids. I took off my left glove and felt the side of his neck. He wasn't dead, just unconscious. I looked at him. This was the moment – the moment I wanted to experience, the moment I had promised myself. I hit him again, hard, driving the edge of the stone deep into the side of his head through the bone. And then he was completely still.

I looked down at the man. A thousand different feelings fought for my attention. I had done it! I felt high, drunk, untouchable. I felt brilliant, strong, undefeatable. I was alive.

I threw the stone far away. Let the police find it, I thought. They would learn nothing from it.

Then I took a playing card out of my jacket pocket, found the dead man's wallet in his jacket and put the card inside. I put the wallet back where I had found it.

A moment later I picked up my backpack and started back to my car.

This is just the beginning. I can show them. I can show them they are wrong. I can show them what I'm really made of.

*　　*　　*

It was four o'clock in the afternoon when Detective Inspector Charles Neville got out of a dark blue police Land Rover in the middle of the cold North Yorkshire moorland near Surrender Bridge. The emergency call reporting a dead body had come in an hour or so earlier. The first police officers had arrived at the scene twenty minutes later and established that the death wasn't natural. Neville had immediately been called out. It was his day off and he had been out with his wife. Shopping for a new kitchen for his home suddenly seemed far less important.

As Neville got out of the vehicle, a young woman with short dark hair came over to him. It was his sergeant, Helen Scott.

'I got here a few minutes ago,' said Scott. 'The body's over there behind that building.' She waved a hand in the direction of an old roofless building that had half fallen down.

Neville could see that black and yellow scene-of-crime tape had already been put around the building, and also round a largish area of moorland. Three other Land Rovers and a couple of other off-road vehicles were parked near the building.

As Neville walked with Scott towards the building, he looked up at the sky. Thick dark cloud was beginning to blow in from the west.

'Yorkshire weather,' he said bad-temperedly, pointing at the sky. 'Let's hope the rain keeps away until we're finished here.'

Neville was from the South-East. Although he'd lived in Yorkshire for the last ten years, he still hadn't got used to the weather. When the sun was out, it was indeed a special place, but it wasn't uncommon to experience all four seasons in one day.

'Yes,' agreed Scott.

Around the corner of the building they found Kay Harding, the police doctor, bending over the body of a middle-aged man dressed in hiking clothes and boots. He still had a backpack on. Harding stood up as she heard the detectives arrive and started talking immediately.

'Charles, Helen,' she said, looking from one to the other and then down at the body. 'What we have here is the body of a fifty- to fifty-five-year-old man. He was presumably out walking. Someone has hit him hard on the side of the head twice. Probably with a stone.'

'Time of death?' asked Neville.

'Somewhere between eight and ten this morning, I'd say,' replied Harding.

'Anything else?' asked Neville.

'Not at the moment,' replied Harding. 'Once the photographer's done his business, I'll take the body away. I'll leave you the backpack and anything I find in his pockets.'

'OK. Thanks,' said Neville. Neville's mood improved. Harding was one of the best – clear, professional, and she didn't waste words. He liked that. He looked at the sky again and then at his watch. They would have to hurry. He turned to Scott.

'We'll have enough daylight,' he said, 'but God knows how long the rain will hold off. Get this area searched – as much as you can and as carefully as you can. We're obviously looking for anything that might be useful, but we're especially looking for the stone that killed him.'

'Right,' answered Scott.

'Who found the body?' asked Neville.

'A local couple,' answered Scott. 'They're in the green Land Rover over there.' She pointed to it.

'I'll go and talk to them,' said Neville. 'Then we'll need to think about an operations room. Reeth is the nearest village. Maybe there's somewhere there.'

Scott nodded. She and Neville had offices at the police station in Richmond, the nearest town, but that was almost twenty kilometres away. Neville would want to be closer to the scene than that. There was a mobile office they could bring over and use, or they could find a large room nearby that they could borrow.

'Right,' she said. 'I'll get the search started here.'

* * *

At eight o'clock the following morning Neville and Scott and a team of fifteen officers met in Reeth Memorial Hall, their new operations room. This large empty room was normally used for anything from children's playgroups, to concerts, to band practice. Now it was filled with desks, chairs, computers, phones and police officers.

Neville stood facing his team, his age showing in the grey of his hair and the lines on his face. Scott was next to him. Neither of them had had much sleep. Behind them was a whiteboard with the photograph of a man's face on it.

'OK,' began Neville. 'First, what we know. This is Matthew Kenworthy.'

He pointed at the photograph.

'He was found at three o'clock yesterday afternoon by a local couple who were out walking their dog. He died some time yesterday morning between eight and ten. Someone hit him on the side of the head twice with a stone. We've got the stone, but it's anyone's guess if we'll find out anything from it.'

He stepped back and looked across at Scott.

'Over to you,' he said.

'Kenworthy was here on his own, on a walking holiday,' she began. 'He was staying at the Shoulder of Mutton pub here in Reeth. He arrived a couple of days ago. He hadn't been to the area before. He was friendly, but kept himself to himself.'

She cleared her throat before continuing.

'Yesterday morning he went off in his car, intending to walk an eight-kilometre path that goes in a circle from Surrender Bridge. We found his car near the bridge.'

Scott then pointed to a number of plastic bags on the table beside her.

'We've been through the things in his room. There's nothing of interest there. We've been through what he had with him on the walk. He just had the usual stuff that walkers take – map, GPS, hat, gloves, sandwiches, water – but there was one unusual thing.'

Scott picked up a plastic bag and held it up so that everyone could see. Inside the bag was a playing card.

'The ace of spades,' she said. 'It was in his wallet. And there were no other cards in his room. Any ideas?'

Heads shook all round the room.

Neville stepped forward again.

'OK,' he said. 'Kenworthy was single and lived in Bristol. The police there are making inquiries. Up here we've got work to do too. I want four of you to walk the eight kilometres that Kenworthy intended to walk. The murderer may have followed him or may have come from the opposite direction. Go in two pairs – one pair in the same direction as Kenworthy, the other pair in the opposite direction. Check along the path for anything that might be useful.'

Neville picked up a pile of photographs from the table and gave them to Scott.

'I want the rest of you making door-to-door inquiries in Reeth,' he said. 'It's a small place. Everyone knows everyone. Take Kenworthy's picture with you. See if anyone knows him, or spoke to him, or saw anyone speaking to him. DS Scott will tell you who's doing what.'

Neville turned and was about to leave the room when a voice came from the back.

'Sir.'

Neville turned round.

'Yes?' he said.

One of the officers had a hand in the air to show that he had spoken.

'What is it?' asked Neville.

'The ace of spades, sir,' said the officer. 'I've just remembered – it's the card of death.'

Chapter 2 *A serial killer?*

I waited ten days before I decided to kill again. I could have waited longer, but I wanted to experience that wonderful feeling again. I wanted to experience it quite badly. That feeling of pleasure, of being successful, and of showing I'm right. I've read the papers and the police seem to have no idea what's happening. I didn't think there was any danger of being found out. I was right about that.

I decided to use the same basic plan as before. I would park my car in one place and then find an 'unwilling helper' somewhere completely different.

However, I had made some improvements to my plan. The first was to leave my car in full view somewhere. Hikers leave their cars all over the North Yorkshire countryside. No-one pays them any attention. But a car that appears to be hidden might now, after what happened ten days ago, be of great interest to the police.

Secondly, I was going to put my plan into action in the late afternoon. I hoped that meant the body wouldn't be found until the next morning. That would make things a little more difficult for the police.

Another change was to use a knife. I had decided I wanted to experience different ways of killing.

Finally, I was going to use footpaths to get to the place I had chosen. There are so many paths all over this part of Yorkshire it would be difficult to avoid them for ever. Of course, the police might be able to match my boots or my clothes to something they found along the path. But I had thought about that. After this and every future adventure I would burn everything that I was wearing or carrying. Clever, aren't I? Cleverer than the police, I think.

I drove up the road from Grinton towards Redmire and left my car on moorland about halfway between the two villages. Then I started walking back over the hill towards Reeth. The day was cloudy, but it was warm for the time of year.

The countryside in the Yorkshire Dales is very beautiful: hills and dales, up and down, wild moorland on the tops of the hills, sleepy villages and farms in the dales at the bottom. To Yorkshire people Yorkshire is 'God's own country'. But I wasn't there to enjoy the natural beauty.

It took me a couple of hours walking through completely empty moorland to reach the place I was looking for – a small building. Normally empty, it was sometimes used by groups of people out shooting birds – but not today. It was right beside one of the main paths in the area with wonderful long views each way up and down the valley.

I took my knife and a map out of my backpack and sat down behind the building to wait. There was always a chance that this late in the day nobody would walk past me. However, that was a chance I was prepared to take.

After about half an hour, I saw a man and a woman in the distance, but they turned off before they reached me and walked down the hill to the river at the bottom. That was lucky because it might have been difficult to kill both of them. I was saving a double killing for the time when I would use a gun.

Shortly after that, I noticed a woman on her own coming from the opposite direction. It soon became clear she was going to come right past me. This time I felt very calm. I knew what to *do. Time seemed to move more slowly. As the woman walked towards the building, I prepared myself and began to look forward to what I was going to do.*

She was still about fifty metres away when I stepped out. I was holding the map in my hand. The knife was in the same hand, but hidden under the map. As I stepped out, I was looking at the map so as not to frighten her. She kept on walking towards me and I looked up. She was medium height, blonde, probably in her thirties.

I smiled at her and looked a bit embarrassed.

'I'm sorry,' I said, waving the map a little, but keeping the knife hidden. 'I seem to be a bit lost. You couldn't show me where I am, could you?'

'Of course,' she said and came over to where I was standing.

She bent to look at the map and I stuck my knife sharply into the left-hand side of her chest.

There was a long, soft noise as the air seemed to leave her body. I looked into her eyes, feeling the moment, enjoying it. A surprised look crossed her face. She tried to speak, but couldn't. I let go of the knife as she fell to her knees, then onto her side. Her eyes closed and she was dead. I stood still for a moment looking down at her. I had done it again! I felt wonderful. God-like. This was better than sex.

Quickly I bent down and pulled the knife out of her chest. I cleaned it on the outside of her jacket, then put it in my backpack. I took out a playing card from my pocket and put it in one of her pockets. Just so that the police would know who had done it.

Then I started the two-hour walk back to my car. Two happy hours in which I could relive the moment.

*   *   *

17

Fiona Russell was in her office in the North Yorkshire Police Headquarters in Northallerton. She had just finished reading a recent report about internet crime and sat back to think about what she had learnt. Although she worked for the police, she wasn't actually a police officer. She was a crime analyst. That meant she was one of the few people who was likely to see everything to do with a particular crime. She read every piece of paper, every interview, every report. She looked for patterns, similarities, differences. She reported her findings to the senior officer in the investigation, and she would make suggestions about what else needed to be done or what further information might be useful.

Just as she sat back, her phone rang.

'Russell,' she said, picking up the phone immediately.

'This is Detective Inspector Neville, North Yorkshire Police,' said the voice, coming straight to the point. 'I'm looking for an analyst with experience of serial killers. Your boss tells me you're the person to speak to.'

Russell felt the hairs on the back of her neck stand up. She had worked on two serial killer investigations before. At the end of each she had been exhausted. Each investigation had been a race against time; a race to stop the killer murdering yet more people. Each investigation had demanded long, patient hours; each had stretched her mind more than she thought possible. Each had, in its own way, given her a new and different way of looking at pain and suffering; but each had brought its own excitement and professional pleasure.

'I guess so,' replied Russell.

'Good,' said Neville. 'At the moment we've only got two murders so, if we're going by the rules, this person isn't yet a serial killer.'

Russell knew that for a killer to become 'serial' the rule was three or more.

'But I don't want to wait for number three,' continued Neville. 'There's no doubt in my mind there will be a third one and more if we don't find him. You'll understand why when you see what we've got so far. I'd like you on the team as soon as possible.'

Russell noticed Neville's use of 'him'. There had been female serial killers – but mostly they were men.

'OK,' answered Russell. 'Where are you?'

'Reeth, Swaledale,' replied Neville.

Russell looked at her watch. 'I can be there in about an hour,' she said.

*   *   *

Ninety minutes later Fiona Russell was sitting at a table at the back of the operations room. Helen Scott was in a chair opposite, giving her a quick overview of the investigation so far. She was already describing the second murder.

'The body was found early this morning on the hillside just outside Reeth,' she said. 'I'll show you where on the map in a moment. It was a thirty-two-year-old woman, Sheila McFadyen. She lived in Richmond. She was a nurse. She worked nights at the local hospital and often came over here during the day to go walking. She was divorced. Her ex-husband lives locally, but they seem to have got on well enough. He says he was at home at the time she was murdered. On his own. It seems unlikely he's our man, but we're checking him out anyway – just to be on the safe side. She didn't have a boyfriend – at least not that anyone knows about. She had a lot of friends. Everyone speaks well of her.'

She held her hands out as if to show the hopelessness of the situation.

'There appears to be no reason why anyone would want to kill her,' Scott added.

She paused for a moment.

'What about the crime scene?' asked Russell.

'Like the first one, we've got almost nothing,' continued Scott. 'The killer stuck a knife straight into McFadyen's heart. We haven't found the knife. The killer pulled it out, cleaned it on her jacket and took it away. We've found nothing at the scene that tells us anything about the killer. We don't know which way he arrived at the scene or which way he left. Actually, we don't know if it's a man or a woman. Nobody seems to have seen anything or anyone strange.'

Scott reached over to a neighbouring table and picked up two small plastic bags. Inside each was a playing card – an ace of spades in one, the two of spades in the other.

'And then we have these,' she said and put them on the table in front of Russell. Russell picked one up and looked at it.

Scott sat back in her chair and looked at Russell.

'Two playing cards,' said Scott. 'The ace was found on the first body, the two on the second. You can see why the boss thinks we've got a serial killer on our hands. Of course, the cards are a common make. Available anywhere.'

'Yes,' said Russell, as she put down the ace and picked up the two. Looking at the two of spades, she noticed two handwritten words in the middle of the card. They read 'By knife'. An icy feeling ran down her back.

She put down the card and looked at Scott. She was in her late twenties, with short dark hair, smartly dressed and clearly intelligent. A useful person to have in this kind of investigation. Everyone needed to be awake and alive to all the possibilities. She was about to speak when a tall man in a suit came towards them. His face was lined and there was a lot of grey in his black hair.

'DI Neville,' he said, introducing himself. 'Call me Charles. You must be Fiona Russell.'

He pulled a chair out from the table and sat down.

'Has Helen told you where we're at?' he asked.

'Yes, she has,' answered Russell.

'And?' asked Neville. 'Any immediate thoughts?'

Russell was unwilling to say too much until she knew more about the investigation. However, being new to the team, she felt she needed to give Neville and Scott something. Having read widely about serial killers, she could make a few general points.

'We can make some intelligent guesses,' said Russell. 'First of all, we're most probably looking for a man. Most serial killers are men. There have been women serial killers but, interestingly, they usually prefer to kill indoors – inside the home or maybe in a hospital – a nurse killing off patients, for example.'

Russell looked at Scott and Neville.

'And I'd guess he's between the ages of twenty-five and forty,' she continued. 'He needs to be old enough to plan and organise this. But when they're over forty, people normally calm down, or they've already been caught and locked up.'

Neville and Scott looked at each other, then back at Russell.

'And he does seem to be organised,' added Russell. 'Organised and intelligent. That's why you've found so little at the crime scenes. He's also carried out the murders well away from any CCTV cameras. We're the most watched country in the world, but out here in the Dales there are very few cameras at all – not many CCTV traffic cameras in towns, hardly any cameras around buildings. And out in the countryside none at all.'

Neville and Scott were listening and watching carefully.

'I'd also say we're looking for someone reasonably local – someone who knows the area,' Russell went on. 'I mean, I'm sure you've thought of this yourselves. Both the murders happened in places where the killer was unlikely to be interrupted. He obviously knows the area well.'

'True,' said Scott, putting her elbows on the table. 'But why? Why have these people been killed?'

'I'm not a psychologist,' said Russell. 'I just study the facts. But, looking at the playing cards, I agree with you that he'll try again. I think you're absolutely right that this is a serial killer.'

She looked at both of them and gave a small smile.

'And, of course, if he keeps killing, we'll catch him. We only need to get lucky once. He has to stay lucky all the time.'

* * *

That afternoon the restaurant at the nearby Half Moon Hotel was full of journalists, both national and local, from the newspapers, radio and TV. Charles Neville, standing and facing the room, had explained the latest developments

– the finding of the second body and how the investigation was moving forward. He didn't much like talking to journalists – in fact he didn't much like journalists – but he knew that there were times when they could help investigations. He had given a short report to keep them happy, but said nothing about the playing cards. It was usual for the police to keep back some information. This unreported information was often useful later.

Now he was preparing to answer questions. With two dead bodies and no idea who the killer might be, he wasn't expecting an easy time. He could see Scott at the back of the room standing and watching. She smiled at him to let him know she was there if he needed her. He nodded his thanks.

'I've just time for a few questions,' said Neville, looking around the room. A few people asked for more information about where the bodies had been found; someone else asked some questions about the dead man and woman. Then a woman at the front spoke.

'Gemma Taylor. Radio Yorkshire,' she said. 'There have been two murders so far. Do you think this is the work of a serial killer?'

Neville took a breath before answering.

'As you know, the two people were killed in very different ways,' he said. 'However, we're obviously keeping an open mind on this question.'

A man near the back raised a hand.

'Jonathan Greene. *London Evening Post*. Isn't it true that a playing card was found at each crime scene? Wouldn't that suggest the same killer for both crimes?'

The room had been reasonably quiet, but now there was complete silence. This was new information. Neville's neck started to turn red. Scott could see that he was holding back his anger. Neville caught Scott's attention at the back of the room. She knew what he wanted and nodded at him.

'I'm afraid I can't discuss exactly what was and wasn't found at the crime scenes,' said Neville.

But Greene wasn't giving up so easily.

'Surely playing cards found at each crime scene would suggest the same killer?' said Greene. 'Possibly even a serial killer.'

Suddenly all the journalists started talking to each other. Two left the room, walking past Scott, taking phones from their pockets as they went.

'This second investigation is less than a day old. We don't yet have a clear idea of how everything at the crime scene might be important,' said Neville. He looked at his watch. 'And now, ladies and gentlemen, I'm afraid that's all I have time for.'

He looked at Scott and nodded, then left the room quickly. There was a lot of noise as the journalists stood up and started to leave. When Jonathan Greene stood up, Scott noticed he was short, rather fat, with thinning light brown hair and a big nose. Not attractive. As he walked past her, she turned and walked along beside him.

'Mr Greene,' she said. 'I'm Detective Sergeant Scott. I'd like to have a word with you.'

Chapter 3 *Early investigations*

What a good idea it was to send a text message to that journalist! Of course, he won't know who it's from. I used a special website – aliamail.com. You can use it to send emails and text messages without anyone knowing where they come from. You have to give a name and an email address when you start using the website, but I gave a false name and I used an internet email service. I also sent the message from an internet café, not from my own computer. Smart, eh?

Naturally, the police will want to talk to everyone who knows the journalist's mobile phone number. That could be hundreds of people. And anyway, the police won't find my name. The journalist has no idea that I know his number. How, in fact, do I know it? Well, that's my secret.

So, soon I will have what I want. The information about the playing cards will be in tomorrow's papers. Then the whole country will know that these achievements are the work of one person. The whole country will see how good I am at what I do, how successful I can be. And then eventually, when I reach my final goal, I will show them that they were wrong. Who are 'they'? They are the people who stopped me realising the one burning ambition I had in life. They are the people who wrongly and unkindly took away the chance I had to achieve something real.

But I'm talking too much and, as the saying goes, 'Actions speak louder than words.' I must get on and plan my next adventure.

First I need some new clothes and boots. I burned the clothes I used last time – as I said I would – and the boots are at the bottom of the River Swale with a heavy stone in each one. I don't want to buy new clothes. Second-hand ones will be much better. There are plenty of shops around selling second-hand clothes. For a start second-hand clothes are cheaper – and after all I'm only going to wear them once; but also no-one will recognise them as being mine. That should confuse the police if they ever get a description of me.

Then I've got to decide the 'how', 'when' and 'where' for my next adventure. The 'how' is easy. This time I want to get up close and personal. A strangling, my hands around the throat of my 'helper'. I want to experience the physical closeness that comes from using my hands rather than a stone or a knife. So far I have always watched life go. This time I want to feel it leave.

As for the 'when', it must be soon, I think. I can't wait much longer. The police are no closer to finding me. I don't have to worry about them. And I have a growing hunger for the excitement of the kill. Or is it a thirst – for blood? To be honest, I don't care. For me it has become like a drug – one which I need more and more.

So there's only one thing left to decide: the 'where'. I'll have to study my map. The Yorkshire Dales is a large area, but fortunately I know it well. It will be easy to find somewhere suitable. You might want to know where, but I'm not going to tell you. You'll find out soon enough. A quiet place for a private meeting.

*   *   *

'I tell you – I don't know who sent it to me.' Jonathan Greene searched through his pockets and finally pulled out a mobile phone. Greene, Neville and Scott were at the back of the Reeth Memorial Hall in a small room which Neville had decided to use for interviews. There were four chairs and a table; the walls were a dull cream colour with some tourist photos of Swaledale on them, and there was a window that looked out onto the back of Reeth Garage.

Greene put his phone on the table and pushed it across to Neville.

'Check for yourself,' he said rather crossly. 'There's no sender's number.'

Neville pushed the phone towards Scott. She picked it up, opened it and started pressing buttons.

'You didn't think it might be a good idea to come and talk to me, the senior officer, about it?' Neville's face was still red with anger, and there was a sharp edge to his voice.

'Come on, Inspector,' replied Greene. He put an elbow on the table and turned his hand over. 'I'm a journalist. I get a text message with information about a murder inquiry – information that the police must already have. Do I go and tell the police something they already know, or do I send in the story so that the *Evening Post* is first with the breaking news? Come on, Inspector! Get real!'

'Don't tell me to get real!' exploded Neville. His fist hit the table hard, his face grew darker. 'This is a murder investigation.' Neville spoke slowly, his voice low and angry, his eyes locked on to Greene's. 'You have what could be, in fact probably is, a message directly from the murderer. You have no idea how important that might be to the investigation. It might lead us straight to the murderer. It might help us save a life, lives even. And yet you don't think that the first thing you should do is bring it to the attention of the police? No, Mr Greene. You get real. Keeping information from the police is a crime – and you know it.'

Neville stopped speaking, but continued to stare at Greene. There was silence in the room. Eventually Greene looked away, embarrassed, even a little shaken by Neville's anger.

Scott looked up for a moment and then continued to examine the phone.

'He's right,' she said to Neville. 'There's no sender number on that message.'

'How easy is it to get your number?' asked Neville. 'How many people have it?'

'Not that many,' replied Greene, looking happier now that the questioning had moved onto easier ground. 'Probably just the people in my phone book. I don't give my number out to that many people. And the newspaper won't give it out.'

Neville looked at Scott.

'We'll want that phone then,' he said. 'Make sure you give Mr Greene a receipt for it and get someone to check everyone in his phone book.'

'But, hey, you can't do that,' said Greene. 'I need my phone.'

'Tough,' said Neville, turning back to Greene. 'It's part of a murder inquiry. Now get out. You're lucky not to be spending the night in jail. And next time – if there is a next time – make sure you do the right thing.'

Greene stood up slowly and, shaking his head, left the room. As the door closed, Neville looked at Scott.

'Check him out too,' said Neville. 'And actually, do it yourself. I want someone experienced on it. I want to know how long he's been a journalist, if he's any good, how long he's been at the *London Evening Post*. Everything. I want to know why the murderer chose to give the information to him. If, in fact, he did.'

Scott looked up sharply.

'You don't think he's ...?' she began.

'Probably not,' replied Neville. 'But it doesn't hurt to be careful.'

*   *   *

Late afternoon the following day, with the second murder less than forty-eight hours old, Russell was called into the interview room to talk to Neville and Scott. A lot of noise was coming through from the main hall. Officers were making phone calls, asking questions, checking information, writing reports. Neville closed the door and the noise level dropped.

'Right,' he said, pulling out a chair and sitting down heavily. 'Fiona, you've been here twenty-four hours now. And you've been through everything. What can you tell us?'

Russell sat down. Scott took out a notebook and kept it in her hand. Russell had a pile of papers, which she put on the table.

'Well, I don't want to raise your hopes too much,' began Russell, 'but there is a line of inquiry that might be useful. Though "might" is the important word here.'

'Go on,' said Neville.

'The Bristol police have been very helpful,' continued Russell. 'They've searched Kenworthy's house, spoken to a lot of his friends and to his employers. Kenworthy worked at one of the universities in Bristol. He was a lecturer in medicine at Avon University.'

29

'And Sheila McFadyen was a nurse,' said Scott.

'Exactly,' replied Russell. 'But there's more. She actually did her nursing training at Avon University.'

'So she could have known Matthew Kenworthy?' said Neville.

'Well, yes.' Russell sounded unsure.

'But …?' asked Neville.

'Like I said,' Russell went on, 'I don't want to raise your hopes. Sheila McFadyen was at university twelve, fifteen years ago. I don't yet know if Kenworthy was there then. He lectured in medicine; she studied nursing. OK, the subjects are similar, but they're completely different courses, so even if they were both there at the same time, they might not have known each other.'

'I see what you mean about "might" being the important word,' said Neville. 'However, it's certainly a line of inquiry that's worth following up.'

'Right,' replied Russell. 'I've emailed the Bristol police a list of questions that they can find answers to there. First thing tomorrow morning I'll have another list of questions that your officers can follow up here.'

'Good,' said Neville. 'Anything else?'

'Not really,' replied Russell. 'As I said yesterday, the killer is organised and intelligent. He's left us very little so far.'

'What about McFadyen's ex-husband?' asked Scott. 'Is there any chance it could be him? He kills someone else first, then his ex-wife, then a third person maybe – so it looks like a serial killing, but actually all he wants to do is get rid of his ex.'

'An unpleasant thought,' said Neville. The smallest of smiles came and went in his eyes. 'But one that's certainly worth considering. Why don't you look into that possibility?'

'OK,' replied Scott and wrote in her notebook.

Neville sat back in his chair.

'Now then,' he said, still looking at Scott. 'What about Mr Greene? Tell us what you've found out about him.'

Scott turned back a few pages in her notebook.

'Apparently Jonathan Greene is a well-known journalist. He works mainly down south on the *London Evening Post*, which explains why I've never heard of him.' Scott looked up from her notes. 'He usually covers crime stories, but he also makes his own investigations into areas where he thinks people have been breaking or bending the law.'

'Such as?' asked Neville.

'I've got a list of some of his more recent stories,' replied Scott, turning over a page in her notebook. 'A lot of his stuff is just straight crime reporting – what happened, who did what, who went to prison, that sort of thing. But at the end of last year he wrote a couple of big pieces. One was on crime in the health service – cleaners stealing drugs and equipment and selling it all on the black market. That resulted in a police investigation.'

'I remember that,' said Neville. 'I didn't realise it was Greene.'

'The other piece was an interview with Jerry Anderson,' continued Scott.

'Who's he?' asked Russell.

'One of the big players in organised crime in London in the 1980s,' answered Neville.

'He'd just come out of prison after fifteen years for bank robbery and murder,' continued Scott, 'and Greene persuaded him to do an interview. He talked all sorts of rubbish about how he had seen the light, given up his life of crime and was going to go straight.'

'Mind you,' added Neville, 'I'm told there's a few million that still hasn't been found from his last bank job, so he can probably afford to go straight.'

'Anyway, I guess that's why Greene's phone number is difficult to get hold of,' explained Scott. 'You wouldn't want Anderson calling you up in the middle of the night. He's not a pleasant character at the best of times.'

'Absolutely,' replied Neville.

Scott looked down at her notes again.

'And there's another big story that he's been working on recently,' she said. 'Unfortunately it hasn't made the newspapers yet, and as a result I haven't been able to find out anything about it. He was away for a couple of weeks at the beginning of the year working on something, but ... well, the people I spoke to either didn't know, or didn't want to tell me.'

'I think you should investigate that further,' suggested Russell. 'It might be worth finding out if that's why he's really up here. I mean, it seems odd for a journalist from a London evening newspaper to be here.'

'He might have come because of the text message,' said Scott.

'I don't think so,' replied Russell. She looked through some of the papers on the table in front of her. 'No,' she continued. 'He only received the message a couple of hours before Charles spoke to the journalists. I made a note of the time.'

'Well, I agree with Fiona,' said Neville. 'You need to find out more about this story of Greene's.'

Just then there was a knock. A woman with short blonde hair opened the door and looked into the room.

'Sorry to interrupt, sir,' she said to Neville. 'Another body's been found. An oldish man. On the Harkerside road, near Scabba Wath Bridge. There was a three of spades in his hand.'

Chapter 4 *A different kind of killing*

I needed luck today. I wasn't absolutely ready for the kill. I'd looked at my map. I had some ideas, but I hadn't reached a final decision on where I was going to find my 'helper'.

Then he found me!

I knew him, of course. He lived near me. I'd seen him around and chatted to him before. I passed him on the street near his house in the middle of the afternoon and said hello. He invited me in for a cup of tea and I accepted.

As soon as we stepped into his house, I knew he was the one. Something in the air seemed different. He was an ex-policeman and he knew something. I was sure of it. I experienced an unusual feeling, partly a warning, partly a call to action.

He turned and started to speak. Immediately I knew what I had to do. He looked in good shape for someone in his early sixties. But I'm young, strong and healthy, and I had the element of surprise on my side. To delay would allow the tiniest possibility of watching my dream die. I couldn't let that happen.

My hands flew forward round his neck. My thumbs pressed hard down on his throat, stopping him breathing. His eyes opened wide and filled with fear as he realised what I was doing.

He fought back. He tried to pull my hands away from his throat, but I was too strong. He hit at my arms, but he was already becoming weak. He reached for my eyes with his fingernails, a last hopeless attempt to save himself.

But I was expecting that. My head shot forward through his hands, my forehead hitting him square on the nose. There was the sickening noise of breaking bone. His hands fell weakly down to his sides, as his face started to turn a kind of bluish purple. A few drops of blood from his nose covered his top lip. His tongue came out. His body became a dead weight in my hands. I let it down gently and laid him on the floor.

Then I sat down next to him. I was breathing hard, my heart going as if I had just run a hundred metres. I could feel the sweat on my face and the fear in my heart. Fear? Or was it excitement?

I took some deep breaths and began to feel calmer. I looked at him. I felt his neck. He was definitely dead.

But I couldn't enjoy the moment as I had hoped. I had a decision to make. I could leave the body here. Or I could take it into the countryside where the other bodies had been found.

I looked round. There was only a little blood. It was all on his top lip and drying fast. There were no obvious signs of a fight. Nothing to show that I had been there. But I'm a planner, a careful planner. I knew that the more I planned, the luckier I would be. So I decided to take the body to the countryside. Sure, the police would realise that the body had been moved – I had watched enough crime shows on TV to know that. But they wouldn't know where the body had been moved from. And that might be important. There might be just some little thing in this room – skin, hair, clothing – that could lead the police to me. But not if they didn't look!

It was a good plan. I felt a wave of pleasure wash over me.

I let myself out of the back door and started to walk home. I would need to steal a car – I obviously couldn't use my car for this. I'd also need a blanket to cover the body in the back of the car, and the three of spades.

* * *

Helen Scott pulled the police Land Rover onto the grass at the side of the road, a few hundred metres from Scabba Wath bridge. On the left-hand side of the road was a dry-stone wall, with fields the other side going down to the river at the bottom of the dale. On the right was grass, moorland and some low bushes with yellow flowers. Sheep were wandering freely over the moorland, as they often do at this time of year. It was early evening, not yet dark, and a light rain was falling.

Scott and Neville got out of the Land Rover and climbed to a group of people standing further up the hillside. Kay Harding, the police doctor, was on her knees examining a man's body. He was lying on his stomach, his head turned away looking up the hillside.

Harding stood up as Neville and Scott arrived.

'One of us,' she said, looking at Neville.

Neville's eyes asked the question.

'Brian Barningham,' said Harding. 'He was an inspector in Leyburn. He stopped work last year just after his sixtieth birthday and moved to Richmond.'

'God!' Neville shook his head in disbelief. 'I know. I was there at his leaving party. I knew him quite well.'

Harding bent down to look at the body again.

'I'm afraid it's not pretty to look at,' she said. 'He was strangled. He was also hit in the face about the time he died.'

'Is it the same ...' began Scott.

'Yes,' replied Harding, straightening up and passing a plastic bag to Neville. Inside it was a playing card. The three of spades. And across the middle of the card were the words 'By hand'. Neville passed it to Scott, who looked at it and gave it back to Harding.

36

'But there is a difference,' said Harding, bending down again for another look. 'The body's been moved.'

'Killed here and just moved?' asked Scott. 'Or killed somewhere else and brought here?'

'Oh, killed somewhere else and brought here,' answered Harding. 'I mean, he's lying on his front now. But after death I'd say he spent a short time on his back and then longer on his side.'

Neville looked at the moorland round about, then down at the roadside.

'Get some scene-of-crime tape,' he said, turning to Scott. 'I want it twenty metres each side of the body, down to the road. No-one else can walk there until that area's been searched.'

'Right,' replied Scott, nodding at a couple of the officers in the group to do what Neville wanted.

'And I mean "searched",' continued Neville. 'Carefully. I want officers on their hands and knees. The killer must have come by car, so look for tyre marks by the side of the road too.'

'OK,' answered Scott.

'Who found the body?' asked Neville.

'A local farmer,' replied Harding. 'First farm on the left, that way.' She pointed down the road to her right. 'He had to get back – said something about his sheep.'

'OK,' said Neville. 'We'll talk to him.'

'Time of death?' asked Scott.

'Some time this afternoon,' said Harding. 'Three or four, maybe. It was quite a warm afternoon before the rain came, so it's not easy to be exact.'

'OK. Thanks, Kay,' said Neville. 'He's all yours.'

'He was divorced,' said Neville, looking at Scott. 'But I guess someone ought to tell his ex. I'll go and do that. I know where she lives. You look after things here and talk to the farmer who found the body. I'll meet you back in Reeth in an hour or so.'

*   *   *

At seven o'clock the following morning, Fiona Russell yawned as she checked her email in the operations room. She'd had three hours sleep. She'd stayed up well into the night reading reports from officers in Bristol, Richmond and Reeth. A new email had come in from Bristol overnight, but it didn't contain any useful information. She'd now seen everything to do with the first two murders and everything that had so far come in about the third. The only thing that seemed odd to her was that the third body had been moved. Why was that? Had he had to move it? And if so, why?

She was just turning these questions over in her mind when the door opened and Neville and Scott came into the room, carrying cups of coffee. Neville was speaking.

'… they're going to go crazy,' he was saying. 'Two murders in forty-eight hours.' He looked at Russell. 'Journalists!' he explained – with feeling. 'As if we didn't have better things to do than talk to them! We have work to do.'

Neville walked through to the interview room and put his coffee on the table.

'The killer's made a mistake,' he said, changing the subject. 'I'm sure of it. He's made a mistake and we've got to make the most of it.' He looked at Russell.

'What do you think about it, Fiona?' Neville asked. 'Moving the body, I mean.'

Russell joined them and they all sat down.

'It is strange,' she replied. She thought for a minute and then looked at Neville.

'Up until now we haven't looked at any CCTV film, have we?' she asked.

'There are no CCTV cameras where the bodies were found,' replied Neville. 'We've got no idea what to look for, or where.'

'We might have now,' said Russell.

'What do you mean?' asked Neville.

'Well, we now know Barningham was killed some time soon after three o'clock. And his body was found at about six thirty.' She put a finger to her lips as she continued to think her idea through. 'Our killer might live in one of the villages in Swaledale or Arkengarthdale, or Wensleydale even. But equally he might live in one of the nearby towns.'

'Where there are CCTV cameras,' said Scott.

'Good thinking,' said Neville. He looked at Scott. 'Get going, Helen. We want all CCTV film from the roads leading out here from both Richmond and Leyburn.'

'And Catterick?' asked Scott.

'Yes,' replied Neville. 'And maybe Barnard Castle too. Also, get someone to keep those journalists off our backs. I'll talk to them later this afternoon if I've got time.'

Scott got up and left the room.

'Any news from Bristol?' asked Neville, turning to Russell.

'It's still possible that Kenworthy and McFadyen knew each other,' answered Russell. 'We now know they were both at the university at the same time. However, the Bristol police haven't been able to establish that they ever actually met.'

'OK,' said Neville. 'Keep on at them. And what about McFadyen's husband? Any news on him?'

'He's in the clear,' replied Russell. 'Helen sent some officers round to talk to his neighbours. One of them saw him putting his rubbish out at the time of the murder.'

'Right,' said Neville. 'I suppose crossing someone off our list is a kind of move forward.'

Russell smiled tiredly at Neville as Scott came back into the room.

'This latest murder does raise a few questions,' said Russell. 'The first is: why did he move the body this time? Also, the fact that Barningham was ex-police – is that important in any way?'

Neville and Scott both shook their heads.

'No idea,' replied Scott.

'The other thing,' continued Russell, 'is: why is he doing this? There has to be a reason, even if it only means something to him. Look at the ways he's killed: hit on the head with a stone, stabbed with a knife, strangled. The first card didn't have any writing on it. But the second and third said "By knife" and "By hand".'

'It's almost as if he's trying out different ways of killing people,' said Scott.

'Exactly,' replied Russell.

There was silence for a moment.

'Maybe to show that he can,' suggested Scott.

More silence.

'He doesn't seem to be getting pleasure from making people suffer,' said Russell. 'I mean, some serial killers take ages – they almost play with the people they kill.'

'So you'd say it's the act of killing that's important to him then, would you?' asked Neville.

'Yes, I think so,' replied Russell.

* * *

Later that morning Scott was walking back from the baker's in Silver Street, after an unsuccessful attempt to buy some cheese sandwiches, when she saw Jonathan Greene walk into the Shoulder of Mutton pub. He had a large bag over his shoulder and was wearing a patterned grey shirt and grey trousers. Given his appearance and build, it wasn't a great fashion choice. He looked a bit like a baby elephant.

'Well, there's always one way to find out what he's doing here,' Scott said to herself. She waited a couple of minutes and then walked into the pub after him.

Greene was sitting in the corner beside a coal fire. There was a glass of beer in front of him and he was reading the *Darlington and Stockton Times*. He looked up as Scott came over to his table.

'A little light reading,' he said with a smile. 'I love local newspapers.' From the way he spoke Scott realised he meant something quite different.

'Not good enough for you, the *D and S*?' asked Scott. 'Not in the same class as the nationals and the London dailies?'

'Hey, I was joking,' replied Greene, looking a little hurt.

'Yeah, right,' said Scott, not believing him for a moment.

Scott pulled out a chair and sat down.

'I'd like to ask you a few questions,' she said.

Greene said nothing. Scott looked him straight in the eye.

'It would be very helpful if you'd answer them here and now,' she said, 'rather than make me take you to the operations room to talk to DI Neville. I think you'd prefer it

41

too. In the inspector's judgement, journalists are the lowest form of human life. You may have noticed.'

Greene smiled.

'Ask away,' he said. 'I can't promise to answer them all. But I never mind talking to an attractive woman.'

Scott felt slightly sick at the thought of being chatted up by Greene, but she continued.

'As you know, we're looking into who could have your mobile number, especially up here in North Yorkshire,' she began, 'so it would be helpful for us to know why you're here.'

'Ah!' said Greene.

'We know you didn't come up here to report on the murders,' said Scott.

'Ah!' said Greene again. He bit his bottom lip, then smiled and said, 'How badly do you want to know?'

Scott wasn't sure if this was a real question or a chat-up line. It didn't really matter to her.

'How badly do you want to see DI Neville?' she asked in reply, looking at Greene. Her eyes were stony.

Greene pushed a hand through what hair he had left.

'This is really difficult ...' he began. 'I mean, I don't tell anyone about my stories until—'

'Where were you earlier this year?' interrupted Scott. 'I understand you were out of the country for a time. Where did you go?'

Greene paused a moment, then seemed to accept that he would have to answer.

'The Middle East,' he said.

'The Gulf?' asked Scott.

'Yes.'

Scott had a sudden thought. The army. Catterick Garrison was about twenty kilometres from Reeth. There were over 12,000 soldiers there, all of whom had seen active service.

'The army,' she said.

'Yes,' said Greene.

'You've been talking to soldiers,' she said. It wasn't really a question.

'Yes,' said Greene.

'We haven't found any soldiers' numbers in your phone book,' said Scott.

'I told you. I don't keep many numbers in my phone book,' he answered.

'But you've given your number to some soldiers,' said Scott.

'Yes,' replied Greene.

Scott took out a notebook and pushed it across the table.

'I want the name of every soldier who has your number,' she said.

'But—'

'Now,' said Scott.

Greene held out his hands.

'I can give you some names,' he said, 'but not all of them. I meet a lot of these guys in pubs. We just chat. I don't ask them their names. Quite often they don't want me to know. With the kind of story I'm investigating, if their name gets in the paper, it makes trouble for them with the army. They have to be careful.'

Scott took out a pen and gave it to Greene. She looked him in the eye and said nothing. Greene pulled the notebook towards him and started writing.

'When you've done that,' said Scott, 'you can tell me exactly what you're investigating.'

Chapter 5   *Caught on film*

I got away with it – but I was exhausted! So tired that this morning I slept till midday. Part of the tiredness was physical – first the fight, then moving the body. Part of the tiredness was in the mind – because I hadn't been completely ready for this adventure I'd had to think quickly. And carefully.

No-one else was at home when I got up. I made a coffee and thought back to yesterday afternoon. I needed to check I had made no mistakes.

I had walked home for a blanket, a change of clothes and the three of spades. Although I was in a hurry, I walked – running would have drawn attention to me. I put the blanket, the card and a pair of binoculars in a bag, and went out to look for a car. Stealing a car is easy when you know how – and I know how.

I drove it back to my 'helper's' house and parked round the back, got the body onto the back seat and covered it with the blanket. Then I started out towards Reeth. On the way I thought about where to leave the body: a side road, somewhere quiet, where I could get the body out without being seen. It was about four o'clock in the afternoon, but a light rain had been falling all afternoon. There wouldn't be many walkers out. I decided on the perfect place.

I drove along the Swaledale road and turned left over Scabba Wath bridge. Then I turned left again onto the road back to Grinton and Reeth. There was moorland here with low bushes that would hide the body for a while. I pulled off the road – there was grass by the side of the road, so I wouldn't leave any tyre marks. Then I got out of the car and carefully checked the countryside around me with the binoculars. Nobody.

Working quickly, I got the body off the back seat. Holding it by the ankles, I pulled it up the side of the hill and hid it behind some bushes. I left the card in the man's hand, looked round to make sure there was nothing for the police to find, and made my way back to the car.

There was little else left to do – get rid of the car, change my clothes and burn the ones I was wearing, drop my shoes in the river. Easy!

It had all been rather hurried, and I was sorry about that. But now that it's over, I can relax, look back and enjoy the moment. I can put a third sticker on my murder map to show where the third body will be found – if it hasn't been found already.

I can also start planning my next adventure. I'm getting a taste for this. Not only can people see how powerful I am and what I can achieve, but I'm also enjoying the feeling. It's the high that comes with every kill, the certainty that it's right to be doing this.

The next one will be two. Double pleasure. I'll use the gun. I've been out on the moors and fired a couple of shots just to get used to it. There are only five shots left in the gun and I don't know if I can get any more bullets. Because of that, I want to get close so there's no chance of missing. I know when and where it's going to happen too. It will be in the early evening, at the roadside. So I'll need to steal another car – but that won't be a problem. Perhaps tonight is a bit early. Or perhaps not. Already I can feel the excitement building. Already I know how good the feeling will be.

Yes. Tonight.

That evening Fiona Russell was at her desk, wondering when she'd next get a good night's sleep. She reached for her coffee and heard another email come through on her computer: a report of two cars stolen in Richmond the afternoon before. Two stolen cars was pretty unusual for Richmond. It wasn't a big town. Cars didn't often get stolen and two on the same day was strange.

A dark green Mini had been stolen from the Market Square late in the evening and a silver Skoda had gone missing from the Gallowfields Business Park some time between 3.15 p.m. and 3.45 p.m. The Skoda had been stolen around the time of the third murder. So – a Skoda then. Maybe.

Russell made a note of the car number. Then she started up some CCTV film on her computer, film from the one camera in Richmond that covered the road out to Swaledale and Reeth. She pressed FAST-FORWARD until the time in the right-hand corner was 15:13:27. That was about the right time, but was it the right road? Of course, the car thief might not be the killer at all. He, or she, might not even have headed towards Swaledale.

Russell hit PLAY. Cars went past. Then cars didn't go past. Then one car. Then no cars for a long time. It wasn't a busy road. She hit FAST-FORWARD, then PLAY again when more traffic came along.

The time got to 16:00:00. The Little Red Bus went past – the bus service from Richmond to Reeth and then on up Swaledale – then a farm vehicle followed by a line of cars, then nothing.

Russell stopped the film and went back. The cars behind the farm vehicle were quite close together. She froze the picture and looked closely. At the back of the line was a BMW, then an Audi, a Ford, a Land Rover, but what was the first car? It was difficult to see. The CCTV was black and white so that was no help.

She zoomed in close and moved down the picture to try and see the car's back number plate. It was hidden – the Land Rover was too close. She went back a couple of minutes and started the film again. This time she played it slowly.

When the cars came into view she froze the film and zoomed in on the back of the first car. Yes! It was a Skoda – that was good. She let the film go forward again slowly. Stop! She could see half the number plate, just the last three letters. They were the same as the last letters of the stolen Skoda. Yes! That was very good!

Something like electricity rushed through her; her head felt light. The feeling almost took her breath away.

Just then Scott came into the room. There was an excited look on her face, but she stopped when she saw Russell.

'Fiona, are you OK?' she asked, looking worriedly at the other woman.

Russell waved a hand and gave her a big smile.

'I'm fine, I'm fine,' she said. 'Come and look at this.'

She took the film back to where the line of cars first came into view.

'Watch this,' she said. 'The first car behind the tractor is the one to watch. I think our man is driving it.'

They watched the film closely until the cars went out of sight. The cars were moving away from the camera so it was impossible to see the drivers. Russell took the film back to the beginning and they watched it again slowly. Then Russell stopped the film and looked at Scott.

'Why do you think it's him?' asked Scott.

'The car was stolen around the time of the murder,' answered Russell.

'Ah,' said Scott. 'You think he stole a car rather than used his own – if he has one.'

'Yes,' replied Russell. She reached out and took hold of Scott's arm. 'If it's him, he stole the car,' she said. 'And he drove out from Richmond – so maybe he lives there.' She smiled at Scott. 'He's starting to make mistakes.'

Russell let go of Scott's arm and stood up.

'Anyway,' she said, 'you came in here with something important.'

'Oh yes,' said Scott, the excited look returning to her face. 'Let's find Charles. We need to compare notes.'

* * *

Half an hour later Neville, Scott and Russell were sitting round the table in the interview room.

'Let me get this straight,' said Neville, looking at Scott. 'The investigation that Jonathan Greene is working on at the moment is to do with the army.'

'Yes,' replied Scott. 'He's looking at the effects of active service on soldiers who have been out in the Middle East and the Gulf – mainly the effects on their minds, and what the government is doing to help soldiers who are badly affected.'

'I thought he was a crime reporter,' said Russell.

'He is,' replied Scott. 'He thinks the government isn't doing enough. Apparently he feels that their position can be seen as criminal. Greene's brother was a soldier. He was so badly affected that he had to leave the army. He now never goes out of his house. For Greene, this is personal.'

'I see,' said Neville. 'And you think a soldier sent Greene the text message about the cards – a soldier that Greene gave his number to.'

'That does seem logical,' said Russell. 'I mean, we think the killer lives locally. We think the killer sent the text message. The killer had Greene's mobile number. And the only people up here that he has given his mobile number to are soldiers and a few other journalists.'

'And how many soldiers did Greene give his number to?' Neville asked Scott.

'That's the problem,' replied Scott. 'He doesn't know. I've got half a dozen names here, but he's talked to lots more. Soldiers are quite happy to talk to him. But because his investigation is unlikely to be popular with the army, they're less happy about giving him their names.'

Neville looked at Russell.

'And you think you have the killer on CCTV in a stolen Skoda, leaving Richmond just after the last murder?'

'Yes,' replied Russell. 'I need to see if he comes back the same way later. I might even get to see him since he'll be facing the camera. But you know how clear CCTV pictures are. I don't expect to be able to tell you what he looks like.'

She opened her mouth to say something else, but then stopped and thought.

'Yes?' asked Neville.

'As far as I know,' said Russell slowly, still thinking her ideas through, 'no cars were stolen around the days of the first two murders. I'll check that, but I'm pretty sure I'm right.'

Neville and Scott said nothing. They waited for Russell to finish making her point.

'That means he must have used his own car to come out here for the first two murders,' said Russell.

'So more than likely he's going to be on CCTV in his own car on those days,' said Scott. 'If they still have the film.'

'They don't use videotapes these days,' said Russell. 'Everything's on computer – hard disk. And it's kept for longer, so we should be able to get hold of it.'

'Right,' said Neville, making a decision. 'Fiona, first check the CCTV to see if you've got him coming back into Richmond yesterday. Then look at the film from the same camera for the first two murders.'

He turned to Scott.

'Helen,' he said, 'you follow up the army idea. You've got the list of soldiers. Go over to Catterick. Talk to them. Ask questions. See if you can find out who else talked to Greene. Take a couple of officers with you. This could be important.'

Pushing his fingers through his hair, Neville stood up.

'It'll be good to have something new to tell the journalists tomorrow,' he said. 'I have to say I'm getting sick of seeing my photo on the front page of national newspapers.'

*   *   *

As Neville, Scott and Russell were making their way back into the operations room, they heard a woman police officer talking on the phone.

'Yes,' she said. 'Yes, I agree that's very strange. Well, I'll tell my boss and …' At that moment she looked round and saw Neville behind her. 'Just a moment. My boss is right here. I'll pass you over.'

Neville raised his eyebrows.

'Inspector Atkins from Richmond. Something about a stolen car,' said the officer.

Neville took the phone.

'DI Neville,' he said. He lifted a hand to tell Scott and Russell to wait. They heard his end of the conversation.

'That's right ... Yes, I know. We've just been talking about it ... Yes, that is strange ... Yes, well, I'd like forensics to examine it as soon as possible. We think it may have been used by the killer ... OK, I'll leave it with you ... Tell them to ring me as soon as they have anything.'

Neville gave the phone back to the officer and looked at Scott and Russell.

'They found the car in almost exactly the same place it was stolen from,' he told them. 'Atkins is getting forensics on to it.'

'Strange to be in the same place,' said Scott.

Russell looked thoughtful. 'I wonder why?' she asked.

'What do you mean?' asked Neville.

'Why did he put it back in the same place?' she asked. 'There must be a reason. It could be close to where he lives – so it was easy to get to. Or it could be a long way from where he lives to make life difficult for us.'

Scott walked over to the door and back, thinking. The others watched her.

'The timing,' she said. 'The timing is important. We know the time of death: soon after three. By four o'clock we've got him on the CCTV camera coming out of Richmond.'

'Exactly,' replied Russell.

'He must have stolen the car from somewhere close to the scene of the crime,' said Scott.

'The car was in the Gallowfields Business Park,' said Russell.

'Not far from Barningham's house,' added Scott.

'Which might be the scene of the crime,' said Neville, 'although we haven't found any signs there.'

Just then a phone rang on the other side of the operations room.

A police officer answered it, then looked at Neville.

'Another one, sir,' he said. 'In fact, this time there are two.'

The room went silent. Russell's eyes opened wide. Neville went across the room and took the phone. After a short conversation he put the phone down and turned to face the room.

'The four and five of spades. By gun,' he said. 'He's shot a young couple out by Surrender Bridge.'

He looked at Scott.

'Let's go,' he said.

'Sir?' asked Russell. She knew they normally used first names, but she was intending to ask for something special. A little extra politeness would be good politics.

Neville looked at her. She could see he knew what the question was. She could also see what the answer would be.

'Yes,' he replied.

'I know the scene of the crime isn't where I'm usually supposed to be ...' she began.

'Yes, yes, come on,' replied Neville. 'Get your coat and come with us. But don't be sick.'

'I have seen dead bodies before,' said Russell.

Chapter 6   *Closing in*

Life just gets better and better. Or is it death that's getting better? Anyway, it was another perfect killing. I'm so good at it. Why they didn't want me, I just don't understand.

I walked down to the old station to find myself a car. The old railway station is now a cinema and there's a car park in front of it. If the owner of the car was watching a film, I might even get the car back before the film finished. He or she wouldn't even know it had been stolen. It would all depend how the evening went.

It was early evening, not dark yet. You might think I was taking chances, stealing cars in broad daylight. But I'm quick. I broke into the car quite easily, put my gun on the floor in front of the passenger seat and got the car started. Then I drove out towards Reeth and Swaledale. I knew what I was looking for – there are small parking areas beside the road in a number of places in the dale. I would drive round until I found one with a car parked in it: maybe an old couple who'd stopped to look at the view or some young lovers having a kiss and a cuddle. It's all the same to me. I just want to show what I can do.

I got to Reeth first. The lights were on in Reeth Memorial Hall. I'd read in the papers that the police were using it as an operations room. It seemed funny to be driving past the place they were trying to catch me from. 'Catch me if you can,' I thought. 'But you can't. You won't.'

There was no-one parked between Reeth and Langthwaite, so I turned left along the road to Surrender Bridge and headed towards Swaledale.

There's a ford along here, where a stream goes over the road and you have to drive through the water. The ford is famous because it was always shown at the beginning of a popular TV series about a vet. I'd watched those programmes as a kid, but these days I only watch crime shows.

From there I drove on to Surrender Bridge. As I came over the top of the hill and looked down towards the bridge, I could see that, just over the other side, a blue car was parked and there were people in it. Two people. Just what I was looking for.

I drove over the bridge and then stopped – but not too close to the other car. I didn't want to alarm them. When I'd stolen the car I'd noticed that there was a map on the back seat. I thought I'd try the map business again.

I put the gun in my pocket and opened the map. Then I got out and walked across.

There was a young couple in the car. He was about twenty, dark-haired, good-looking; she was the same age, blonde and pretty. They had been kissing, but had broken off when I stopped my car.

Seeing me coming towards them, map in hand, the young woman opened the driver's window.

'Can I help you?' She smiled at me.

I was only a couple of metres away by then. I smiled back, took out my gun and shot her in the head. She fell forward onto the wheel.

Her boyfriend shouted something, but he didn't have time to do anything. I pointed the gun a few centimetres to the left and shot him through the head as well.

I checked they were both dead and then sat both the bodies up in their seats so they looked alive. Finally I reached into the car and threw the four and five of spades onto the back seat.

When you fire a gun like this, the bullet shoots out of the front of the gun and the casing, which holds the bullet, is thrown out of the side, sometimes a few metres away. One casing was easy to find. I picked it up and put it in my pocket. The other was nowhere to be seen. I searched for it among the grass and small bushes, but I just couldn't find it.

After a few minutes I heard the sound of a car in the distance. It was time to go. Even if the police found the casing, it was unlikely to matter. Taking the casings was just me being careful, leaving nothing to chance. What the police really needed was the gun. With the gun and the bullets they could get a match. But they would never find the gun.

I got back in my car and drove away.

It would be some time before the bodies were found. Nobody would think twice about gunshots out here. Farmers are always shooting rabbits, and the rich pay large amounts of money to come and shoot birds. The sound of gunshots isn't unusual in the Dales.

I drove back to Richmond enjoying the moment, feeling the excitement run through my body and already looking forward to the next killing. I'm getting closer to my goal.

* * *

It took Neville, Scott and Russell fifteen minutes to reach Surrender Bridge from the operations room in Reeth. Neville and Russell went in a police Land Rover; Scott took her own car. Black and yellow scene-of-crime tape was already closing off a wide area around a small blue car. Two police Land Rovers were parked on the opposite side of the road behind a red Toyota 4x4. A man and a woman police officer were talking to someone in the Toyota. A third police officer was setting up some large lights so that everyone could see what was going on. A fourth was standing just near the scene-of-crime tape.

'The police doctor's on her way,' he said as Neville came up to him.

Neville nodded towards the Toyota.

'What's happening there?' he asked.

'The young woman's mother,' replied the officer. 'Her daughter was out with her boyfriend and said she'd be home for dinner by eight. When she wasn't back by ten thirty, her mum came out looking for her. She said she knows the places they usually go. We've been trying to calm her down, but understandably she's really upset.'

'Husband?' asked Neville.

'A couple of the guys have gone to get him, and to tell the boy's parents,' replied the officer.

'The cards?' asked Neville.

'On the back seat,' replied the officer. 'I haven't touched anything. As soon as I saw the bodies and the cards, I closed the area off.'

'Good. Thank you.' Neville turned to Scott. 'Let's have a look.'

They took some white plastic overshoes out of the back of the Land Rover and put them over their own shoes. Then they bent under the police tape and slowly and carefully walked over to the blue car.

'What do you think?' asked Neville and they walked round the car looking in through the windows.

'I'd say they were shot from fairly close,' said Scott. 'But I guess we should wait and see what Kay has to say.'

Just then a green Land Rover arrived and Kay Harding got out. She immediately put on overshoes and joined Scott and Neville. She reached in through the car window and felt the necks of both the young people for signs of life.

'No surprises there,' she said. 'But I have to check.'

Then she bent down and looked at the bullet holes in their heads.

'They were shot from less than a metre away,' she said. 'Let me get on with things and I'll tell you more when I've finished here. I realise how important this is.'

'Thanks, Kay,' said Neville.

Neville and Scott made their way back outside the police tape, where Russell joined them.

'Charles?' she began.

Neville looked at her in reply.

'If he came from Richmond again ...' She left the sentence unfinished.

'Good thinking,' said Neville, looking at his watch. 'Let's say he took some time to find what he was looking for. So first see if there are any reports of stolen cars. Then check CCTV film from about six o'clock to eleven o'clock. You know what to look for.'

* * *

Russell had a busy night. To start with, no cars had yet been reported stolen. The next problem was that CCTV cameras in North Yorkshire weren't managed by the police, but by a local government officer. He wasn't happy to get a midnight phone call from Fiona Russell wanting CCTV film from that evening and from two weeks earlier.

'Can't it wait until morning?' he complained sleepily.

'Sure,' replied Russell. 'I'll suggest that to my boss. I'm sure he'd be happy for you to come into the police station until then. Helping us with our inquiries. Through the night.'

'God!' thought Russell, smiling to herself. 'I've spent so long with police officers I'm starting to sound like one.'

Russell received the film by email within the hour and started work. First she played through the film from the evening before, noting the number of each car or van that went from Richmond towards Reeth and Swaledale. Then she went through again noting cars going back into Richmond. Then she matched the two lists. Ten cars were on both lists. She yawned, pushed her fingers through her hair and looked across the operations room. Neville and Scott had returned at two in the morning. They were in the interview room working their way through a pile of papers.

Russell poured herself a coffee from the machine by the window and went back to her computer. There was no point telling Neville anything until she had names and addresses for the owners of those ten cars. In any case, she felt sure the killer had used a stolen car.

After half an hour on the Driver and Vehicle Database, Russell had the information she needed. She went over to join Neville and Scott in the interview room. They looked up as she came in.

'Ten names and addresses,' she said, putting a piece of paper on the table. 'Owners of cars that left Richmond early yesterday evening in the direction of Reeth and returned some time later. They're all possibles. But my guess is the car was stolen, even though it hasn't yet been reported. Anyway, I'll start on the film from the first two murders now.'

Just then the phone rang. Neville picked up.

'DI Neville.' He listened for a moment then said, 'Just a moment, Kay. Helen and Fiona are here. I'll put you on speakerphone.'

He pressed a button and Kay Harding's voice came into the room loud and clear.

'You owe me, Charles,' she said. 'I've been working through the night on this one for you.'

'Noted,' replied Neville. 'What have you got?'

'I can narrow the time of death to between eight and nine thirty, if that helps,' she answered.

'It might,' replied Neville.

'They were both young and healthy. Both, as you know, died from a bullet wound to the head,' continued Harding.

'OK,' said Neville. 'And the bullets?'

'Yes, the bullets,' said Harding. 'Both from the same gun. Both nine-millimetre. Both made in Iraq.'

'What?' Neville half-shouted the question. 'What do you mean?'

'Your guys found a casing from one of the bullets at the scene of the crime,' explained Harding. 'There was some writing on it. I copied it and emailed it to a friend of mine at Newcastle University. He's a lecturer in Middle Eastern Studies. He told me that the writing was Arabic and that it says "Al-Qādisiyyah". I looked it up on the internet.'

'And?' asked Neville.

'Al-Qādisiyyah is a province in southern Iraq,' said Harding, 'but it's also the name of a factory that makes a nine-millimetre gun called a Tariq – basically a Beretta M1951, but made in Iraq. They've been making them since before 1990 and they're still used today by the Iraqi police.'

'The Iraqi police!' There was disbelief in Neville's voice.

Russell put a hand on his arm.

'No,' she said. 'It adds up. It's all to do with the army. Soldiers out in Iraq or Afghanistan, or wherever, they get lots of opportunities to get their hands on guns, bullets, knives, all sorts of things – especially from the people they are fighting.'

'Thanks very much, Kay,' said Neville, switching the phone off, deep in thought. He turned to Russell.

'So you're saying,' he said, that it's easy for a soldier to get hold of a Tariq nine-millimetre and bring it back to Britain, as a kind of war prize.'

'Absolutely,' said Russell. 'I worked on a case in London a few years ago where an ex-soldier was selling guns to criminals – guns that he'd brought back from places all around the world.'

Nobody spoke for a moment.

'We come back to soldiers and the army again,' said Neville. He looked at Scott. 'How are you getting on with Greene's list?' he asked.

'I called Catterick earlier,' she said. 'There were six names on Greene's list. Of those, three were at the garrison at the time of the first two murders. And the other three have recently gone out to Afghanistan. They left before the murders started. However, I did manage to speak to one of the first three soldiers. He's given me the names of nine others who spoke to Greene, but didn't tell him who they were.'

Scott looked at Neville and Russell.

'But don't get too excited,' she warned them. 'I get the feeling Greene spoke to a lot more people.'

'Never mind that,' said Neville. 'It's a start. As Fiona said at the beginning, we only need to get lucky once.'

'I don't suppose you found out which of those nine live in Richmond, did you?' asked Russell. 'That's where the cars have been stolen from.'

Scott started to look through the papers on the table in front of her and pulled out the one she was looking for.

'Yes,' she replied, 'I did.' She looked at the list. 'Two of them.'

She turned the paper round so that the others could read it.

'I'll look on the Driver and Vehicle Database to see if either of them has a car,' said Russell. 'Then if we look at the CCTV from the days of the first two murders, we might find a match.'

'Do it,' said Neville and he looked at Scott. 'And, Helen, give Fiona a hand. I've got a feeling we might be getting close.'

* * *

Ten minutes later Russell gave Scott a piece of paper with letters and numbers written on it.

'Two car numbers,' she said. 'One for each of the soldiers who live in Richmond. I've emailed the CCTV film from the day of the second murder to your computer. You look through that. I'll look at the first one.'

'You were right about a car being stolen last night,' said Scott as she sat down. 'It was reported at ten twenty last night in Richmond. The report's only just made it onto the computer.'

Russell thought for a moment.

'Has the car been found yet?' she asked.

'I don't think so,' replied Scott.

'Tell them to try the Gallowfields Business Park,' said Russell.

When Scott looked questioningly at her, Russell said, 'Just a guess.'

Then she pushed her fingers through her hair and took a deep breath. She looked at the two names and addresses on the paper in front of Scott.

'I don't know Richmond that well,' she said. 'Is either of these addresses near the Business Park?'

'Neither of them is very far away,' answered Scott.

Russell sat down in front of her computer. She put her elbows on the table and rested her chin on her hands. She thought for a few moments.

'I think,' she began, speaking slowly. 'I think that the third murder – the one where he first stole a car – I think that maybe it wasn't planned as well as the others. I think he was surprised in some way.'

Scott looked at Russell.

'I also think,' continued Russell, 'that he felt he had to move the body in a hurry. And that first stolen car was taken from the Business Park because it's close to where he lives. Leaving the car there when he'd finished with it was just an attempt to confuse us.'

'That sounds a reasonable guess to me,' replied Scott.

'OK,' said Russell, having another look at the car numbers in front of her. 'Let's see if we can find one of these two.'

Russell and Scott started watching the different films on their computers.

Forty-five minutes later Russell watched the same thirty seconds of film for the third time. Then she sat back in her chair.

'Got you,' she said quietly.

Chapter 7 · *The Reid family*

After the shooting I wanted to put the car back in the station car park. But as I got near, I could see a police car, and a man and a woman talking to two police officers. I drove by quickly, before they saw me. Then I went up to the Gallowfields Business Park. If I leave all the stolen cars in the same place, the police won't know what to think.

I walked home, thinking about the shooting. It was cleverly done in my opinion: a foreign gun, a stolen car, two clean kills. Two killings nearer my goal. I'm like a well-oiled machine, a well-oiled killing machine. Training – ha! I don't need training for this. This is all down to planning, organisation and being brave enough to believe I can do it. Being brave – that's it. They never really thought I was brave enough.

Before I went home, I turned down a side street and decided to keep walking. I didn't want to arrive home and have to talk to anyone. Also I had to put the gun back in its hiding place. I would stay out for another half an hour until everyone at home had gone to bed.

While I walked I could plan my next adventure. It should be soon. Maybe even tomorrow. The sooner I reach my goal, my target number, the sooner I can show the world what I'm made of, and the sooner they'll want me.

Tomorrow, then. Tomorrow morning. A drowning, I think. There are plenty of paths by the river in both Swaledale and Arkengarthdale. It should be easy to surprise someone, hold them under the water and feel the life leave their body. Of

*course, they would fight back, but I would be prepared for this.
I could either knock them out first and then hold them under. Or
I could choose someone smaller and less powerful than me. I
considered both courses of action. I liked them both. I would
decide tomorrow.*

*And where do I plan to do this? Mentally I worked my way
along the River Swale from Reeth to the upper dale. There's
a favourite place of mine where a stream called Barney Beck
joins the river. I had many picnics there as a child; I've walked
that path many times as an adult; I know the place better than
the back of my hand.*

*It was ten past eleven when I let myself quietly in through
the front door. I stopped inside the door and listened. Silence.
Gently I locked the door and went into the kitchen. From there
a door leads through to the garage.*

*The garage is full of everything that we don't want in the
house: old boxes, a clothes dryer, two bikes, a television that
doesn't work, suitcases, all sorts of rubbish. The suitcases
are kept on a kind of platform under the roof. I climbed up and
opened one of them. Inside was a metal box. And in the metal
box was a piece of material. I took the gun out of my pocket,
put the material round the gun, the gun in the box, and the box
back in the suitcase. That's where he keeps the gun – but he
doesn't know that I know!*

*I'll put a sticker on my map tonight for tomorrow's adventure.
You may think that's overconfident of me. But I don't think so. I
know I won't fail.*

* * *

'Major Alan Reid,' said Fiona Russell, writing on a piece
of paper, 'owns a red Ford Focus, KV06EUU. I've got the
car driving out of Richmond towards Swaledale at five

twenty-five on the morning of the first murder and then back into Richmond at eleven forty.'

Helen Scott looked down her list of car numbers.

'I've got the same car at four thirty in the afternoon on the day of the second murder,' she said.

'We've got a match, Charles,' Russell called to Neville.

Neville came over to Russell's desk.

'Address?' he asked.

Russell gave him the piece of paper she had been writing on.

'Quarry Road, Richmond. Is that near the Gallowfields Business Park?' she asked.

'Very close,' said Neville. He looked at Scott. 'Come on, let's go,' he said. He turned to Russell. 'You too. I want to know what you think.'

Half an hour later, at seven thirty in the morning, Scott stopped the police car outside a smart-looking stone house on Quarry Road. The front garden was tidy and well kept. There was no red Ford Focus on the drive in front of the house, nor in the street. Neville, Scott and Russell went to the front door. Neville rang the bell.

There was the sound of someone coming to the door and then the door being unlocked. The door was opened by a white-haired woman in her sixties, wearing a dressing gown over her nightclothes.

'Yes?' she asked.

Neville held up his police ID.

'DI Neville, North Yorkshire Police,' he said. 'This is DS Scott and this is Ms Russell, a police analyst. We're looking for a Major Alan Reid.'

The woman looked worried.

'Alan?' she asked. 'What do you want him for?'

'I'm afraid I can't tell you that,' said Neville. 'Perhaps we could come in.'

The woman opened the door wider.

'Well, yes,' she said. 'I suppose you'd better. Come into the front room and I'll go and get Alan.'

The woman showed Neville, Scott and Russell into a bright room at the front of the house. They stood and looked round it: comfortable furniture, pictures of the dales, family photos, a grandfather clock in the corner.

'Alan!' They heard the woman shout upstairs. 'There are some police officers here to see you. Are you OK coming down on your own?'

'I'm fine, Mum,' was the reply.

There was the sound of someone slowly coming downstairs. Then the door opened. The woman came back into the room followed by a man in his early thirties moving very slowly. Under each arm was a crutch to help him walk. His right leg was normal. His left leg was missing, the trouser leg cut off above the knee.

He looked round the room.

'You'll excuse me if I sit down,' he said. He made his way to a brightly coloured armchair, dropped into it and laid his crutches on the floor beside it.

'Roadside bomb. Afghanistan,' he said by way of explanation. 'I was the lucky one. It killed two of my men. I'm waiting for a new leg.'

Neville, Scott and Russell looked at each other. This man obviously wasn't their killer.

'What can I do for you?' asked Reid, looking at Neville.

'You're Major Alan Reid,' said Neville.

'Yes.'

'You own a red Ford Focus,' said Neville.

'Yes.'

'Where is it?' asked Neville.

'Isn't it in front of the house?' asked Reid.

'No, it isn't,' said Neville.

'Well, Terry's probably gone out in it,' replied Reid.

'Terry?' asked Neville.

'My brother,' explained Reid.

Russell noticed a photo on a small table beside her. Two young men and an older woman: Alan and Terry Reid and their mother. She picked the photo up and passed it to Neville.

'Is your brother in the army too?' asked Neville, looking at the photo.

'No, he's a gardener. Part-time. He works for a few people in different parts of Richmond,' answered Reid.

'Have you been to Iraq as well as Afghanistan?' asked Neville.

'Yes,' replied Reid. 'Twice.'

'Do you own a gun?' asked Scott.

'No,' replied Reid. 'Obviously I know how to shoot one. And I have one with me when I'm on active service. But when we're back home we're not allowed to take guns out of Catterick Garrison.'

There was a short silence.

'What about a Tariq nine-millimetre?' asked Scott.

'What do you mean?' asked Reid.

'I mean, something you brought home to remind you of your time in Iraq. A war prize,' said Scott.

'Major Reid,' said Neville, before Reid had time to answer, 'we're investigating the series of murders in the Dales. You will have read about them in the papers and seen the news reports. I expect an honest answer from you.'

Reid took a deep breath.

'Yes,' he said. 'I do have a Tariq nine-millimetre. But so, I'm sure, do a few hundred other soldiers and ex-soldiers. Mine is well hidden and hasn't been used since I brought it back.'

'Where is it?' asked Neville. 'We'd like to see it.'

Reid picked up his crutches and with difficulty stood up.

'I'll show you,' he said.

Neville nodded at Scott and she followed Reid out of the room.

During the conversation Russell had been looking round the room. She'd noticed more family photos and started to take a closer interest in them: a baby, a young boy and their parents; two teenage boys; two young men and their mother; a younger Alan Reid in army uniform. In fact there were three or four of Reid in uniform, but no recent photos of his brother.

Russell looked at Reid's mother, who had been sitting on the sofa, but taking no part in the conversation.

'Mrs Reid,' she began, 'is Terry younger than Alan?'

'Yes,' answered Mrs Reid. 'There's four years between them.'

'And did Terry want to join the army too?' asked Russell.

'Oh yes,' answered Mrs Reid. 'Once Alan was in the army, it was all Terry talked about – how they'd be in the army together. He always wanted to do what Alan did. You know, he looked up to him like younger brothers often do.'

'So what happened?' asked Russell.

'Well, he started the training,' said Mrs Reid, looking down at the floor, 'and then the army decided they didn't want him.'

Russell said nothing. She just looked questioningly at Mrs Reid.

Eventually the white-haired woman looked up at Russell.

'They said it was something to do with his mind. Something psychological,' she said. 'I didn't really understand it. He's healthy. Strong. He passed all the physical tests. He passed all the exams. And then they said he was "unsuited to life in the modern army".'

'How did he feel about that?' asked Russell.

'Well, you can imagine,' said Mrs Reid. 'Joining the army had been his life's ambition. His dream. And it just disappeared overnight. It was terrible for him. He was very, very disappointed – more than disappointed, actually. Angry, as well.'

Russell looked at Neville and then back at Mrs Reid.

'Do you think it changed him at all?' she asked. 'Not getting into the army.'

Mrs Reid thought about this for a moment.

'Yes,' she said. 'I think it did really. He used to be more open, more friendly with people. He's more private now. He's kind of turned in on himself.'

Just then the door of the front room opened and Scott came back into the room, Reid behind her. There was a gun in Scott's hand.

'A Tariq nine-millimetre,' she said. 'And it's been used recently.'

Mrs Reid made a sound and her hand went to her mouth.

'You can't think …' she began. But she couldn't finish.

Reid's face was white. He looked shaken.

'It can't be Terry,' he said. 'He doesn't know I've got the gun. I've never told him about it. He's not …' He too found himself lost for words.

'We'd like to look in his room,' said Neville.

'Of course,' said Mrs Reid, her voice shaky. 'It's at the top of the stairs on the right.'

Neville gave Scott a sign that she should stay with the Reids. Then he and Russell headed up the stairs.

'We need to find him as soon as possible,' said Russell, as she climbed the stairs behind Neville. 'I think he's gone out to kill again.'

'Today?' said Neville.

'Yes,' replied Russell. 'Today. As a rule, once serial killers get started, the time between the killings gets shorter and shorter. It becomes like a drug. They need it more and more.'

Terry Reid's room was unnaturally tidy: a perfectly made bed, chair and desk arranged with mathematical neatness, pens and pencils in a line, bookshelves with books arranged in order of size, a clothes cupboard.

Neville opened the cupboard door. Russell started on the desk drawers. Two minutes later she was opening out a map she'd found in the third drawer down.

'Here,' she said. Neville came across to look.

'Look where the blue stickers are,' said Russell, pointing at the map. 'The first murder. The second. The third. The fourth and fifth.' Each sticker was at the place where one of the murders had happened.

'And an extra one here,' said Neville, pointing at another. 'Barney Beck. That must be where he's gone.'

Chapter 8 *Catching the killer*

I left the house early this morning. It was cloudy, but it looked as though the sky would clear later. I took Alan's car today. I don't want to steal a car too often. The science is so good these days you can never tell what the police might be able to find. I drove to Reeth and parked in the middle of the village. Then I started out towards the little stream called Barney Beck. The path goes across the fields down to the River Swale, then along the river bank, through some trees.

Just before Barney Beck, the path moves in closer to the river. There's a dry-stone wall on the right of the path and the river is just a couple of metres to the left, with tall trees growing on both banks. So here I am now at the place where Barney Beck joins the river. Waiting.

It's a private place. That's why I've chosen it. And because there are stepping stones across the stream.

Mum often brought Alan and me here when we were young. We'd walk from Reeth and stop here for a picnic and throw stones in the water. Then we'd either return the way we'd come or, when we were older, we'd walk on to Scabba Wath Bridge and back to Reeth on the other side of the river. Happy days.

My dad died when I was eighteen months old, so I didn't know him at all. Alan hardly remembers him either. Mum brought us up on her own. I always felt I was her favourite even though she was very fair. Alan was always out with his friends playing football or cycling or rock climbing or … doing something. I spent a lot of time with Mum. We've always been very close.

I look both ways up and down the river. No-one is coming yet. I find a place where I can hide behind the wall. If a couple or a group of walkers come past, I'll hide. I'm waiting for someone on their own.

Although I'm Mum's favourite, I've always been jealous of Alan. He's the successful one out of us. Mum was so pleased when he got into the army I knew that I had to try too.

I look both ways again. I can see a group of four people in the distance coming along the path from Reeth. Quickly I get into my hiding place. It takes the group fifteen minutes to arrive and go past. I give them another five minutes to get well away. Then I come out for another look in both directions. No-one.

Everything went well when I started my army training. There was nothing physically wrong with me. I passed my exams. Actually, I passed them well. But then there were psychological tests: questions which didn't seem to have a right or wrong answer; questions about being on active service, about being on the front line. And then they told me I was unsuitable. At first I couldn't believe it. Being a soldier was the only thing I wanted. The army had refused me – how would I be able to look at myself in the mirror every morning? I did the only thing I could. I decided to show them they were wrong.

I look both ways along the river again. There's something red about a hundred metres away. I look through my binoculars. It's a woman in a red anorak. She's coming along the path from Scabba Wath. She's on her own.

I stretch my hands open and closed.

This is it.

I'm ready.

*   *   *

Scott drove. Neville and Russell sat in the back of the car. Neville took out his phone and made a call. Russell listened to him giving instructions for a minute, then reached forward and took a map off the front seat. She knew where Barney Beck was – along the River Swale between Reeth and Healaugh – she had walked there many times herself. But she wasn't sure of the easiest way to get to it. She opened the map.

From what Neville was saying on the phone it was clear to Russell that he knew the area well. She stopped listening as she looked at the map. The path from Reeth to where they thought Terry Reid might be was a long one. It would be quicker to park on the road just outside Healaugh and walk down through two fields. She was about to point this out to Neville when she heard him say, 'I want three men, armed, waiting in Reeth, in a car not a Land Rover. We'll pick them up as we go through. The closest we can get to Barney Beck is the road just outside Healaugh. Then we'll go on foot from there.' He turned off his phone.

Russell looked at Neville. His face looked tired, exhausted even, but now there was the light of excitement in his eyes as they closed in on their man. It had been like this with the other serial killer investigations she had worked on. The killings got closer and closer together in time; the police worked longer and longer hours, looking at more and more information; and then everything seemed to explode into madness towards the end.

Scott had the blue light going and made it from Richmond to Reeth in seventeen minutes. An unmarked police car was waiting opposite the Buck Hotel. She stopped beside it and Neville opened his window.

'Follow us,' he told the driver.

Five minutes later they pulled as far into the side of the road as they could, just outside the village of Healaugh. Russell realised why Neville had asked for a car, not a Land Rover. The Land Rover was a high vehicle and you'd be able to see the roof from down by the river, over the top of the dry-stone walls. Clever.

The police officers and Russell got out of the cars. Guns were handed to Neville and Scott. Neville looked at Russell.

'You stay here,' he said. 'You're not police. I don't want you anywhere near this.'

'No problem,' she said. She hoped that with her help Neville and Scott had got to the right place in time to save someone's life. But she was quite happy not to get any closer than this to a serial killer.

*   *   *

Scott opened the gate and the five officers entered the field. She closed the gate. There were a few sheep on the far side of the field and, even with a killer running free, the farmer wouldn't be happy if they got out.

Quickly the officers made their way across the field, keeping low so that they wouldn't be seen. At the bottom of the field was another gate. Opening and closing it quietly, they ran across the next field to the wall at the bottom. They stayed low when they reached the wall. Scott looked round. Faces were set, lips pressed together, guns at the ready.

Neville nodded at Scott. She looked over the wall. It took her five seconds to realise what was happening. There were stepping stones across Barney Beck. A man was standing on one side of the stream. His back was towards her, but she was sure that it was Terry Reid. On the other side of the stream was a walker, a woman in a red anorak. She was a few metres away from the stepping stones and walking towards them. Reid put out a hand to help her over the stones. She took the offered hand. As she did so, she looked up and saw Scott.

Reid realised there was someone behind him. He turned suddenly and looked straight at Scott.

There was no time to think about what to do next. Scott lifted her gun over the wall and pointed it at Reid.

'Police!' she called. 'Let go of that woman's hand and don't move.'

Reid moved fast. He stepped quickly across the stream towards the woman, pulling the hand he was holding up behind her back and putting his other arm round her neck.

'Stay there,' he called to Scott. 'Don't come any closer.'

Scott knew that Neville could hear the conversation. Whispering and pointing, he would be sending the other officers to come up on Reid from behind – probably one to cross the river further back towards Reeth; the other two to go back up towards the road and to get behind Reid that way. She knew he'd stay hidden behind the wall.

'Don't do anything stupid,' said Scott. 'Just let her go and we'll talk.'

'Ha!' Reid laughed and started to move backwards. There was a wall and an opening into a field behind him. Scott could see what he was trying to do, but there was little she could do to stop him.

Suddenly Reid picked a stone off the top of the wall and hit the woman over the head with it. As she fell, he turned and ran fast up the field.

'Quick,' shouted Scott to Neville and the others, as she ran across the stepping stones to the injured woman. 'He's getting away. Towards the road.' Neville turned and started running.

*   *   *

At first Fiona Russell sat in the car, but it soon grew too warm in the autumn sunshine. She got out and stood by the gate that Neville, Scott and the others had first gone through. Her elbows were resting on the top of the gate and she was looking down towards the river. There had been some shouting a few minutes ago, but no shots. She wondered if they'd found Reid or not. A couple of minutes later she saw two of the officers from Reeth climbing over the dry-stone wall down the right-hand side of the field. It looked as if they'd certainly found someone.

She was about to go back to the car when she felt something hard stick into her back.

'Be very careful,' said a voice. 'This is a gun. And I don't want to use it.'

Russell felt sweat break out all over her body.

'What do you want?' she said. She knew it was Reid.

'Are the keys in the car?' asked Reid.

'I think so.'

'Open the passenger door and get in very slowly,' he said.

Russell turned a little to reach the car door. She couldn't see the gun, but she could feel it pressed hard into her side.

Out of the corner of her eye she could see him, the man she had been hunting. He was tall. He looked tired. He had small eyes, a weak chin and straight black hair.

'Take it easy,' she said. 'I'm not a police officer. But I can help you.'

'Don't talk,' he replied. 'Just move very slowly and get in the car.'

Gently, Russell let herself down onto the passenger seat. Reid kept the gun tight against her side.

'Now move across to the driver's seat,' ordered Reid.

Russell was about to move over when she heard a noise. She looked to her left. Neville and Scott had appeared at the gate into the field, guns in hands.

'Leave her alone,' said Neville, his gun pointing at Reid. 'Step back very slowly or we'll shoot.'

'I'll shoot too,' said Reid. 'I'm sure you don't want this woman to die.'

Russell saw Neville and Scott look at each other.

'Where did you get the gun, Reid?' asked Scott. She stared at Reid, then she turned and her eyes met Russell's.

'Fiona, has he really got a gun?' she asked.

Russell thought quickly. She'd felt the gun, but she hadn't seen it. It wasn't the Tariq-nine millimetre – they'd seen that in his house earlier that morning. Did he have another gun? Should she take a chance? She turned sideways and pushed Reid hard in the chest with both hands. He fell away from the car onto his back. In his hand was a piece of wood that he had been pretending was a gun.

Within seconds Neville and Scott were through the gate. Neville pressed his gun to the side of Reid's head; Scott pulled his arms roughly behind his back and put the handcuffs on.

Reid started to fight against the handcuffs.

'Let me go!' he shouted, turning his head from side to side. 'I need to finish this. I need to reach my goal. I need to show them what I can do.'

Neville, Scott and Reid looked at each other.

'The army,' continued Reid, still trying to get his hands free. 'I need to show them I've got what it takes. I need to show them I can kill people. And that I'm good at it. I need to show them I'm just the sort of person they want.'

Neville just shook his head.

*   *   *

Later that afternoon Neville, Scott and Russell were in the bar at the Half Moon Hotel. Reeth Memorial Hall had been emptied of all the desks, chairs, computers and phones that the police had brought. Terry Reid had been interviewed, taken to Richmond police station and would be interviewed again later. Helen Scott had been to Richmond to talk again to Reid's mother and brother. She had then returned to Reeth. Neville had spoken to the journalists and been interviewed for TV and radio.

Neville carried three glasses from the bar and put them on the table where they were sitting: beer for him, white wine for Scott, red wine for Russell.

'Thank God that's over,' he said, sitting down heavily.

'Yes,' agreed Scott.

'And just because the army refused him,' said Neville.

'Well, in his eyes the army refused him because they didn't think he could kill people,' explained Russell. 'He killed to show that he could. And he used a different way of killing each time to show how good he was.'

'Crazy,' said Neville. 'Completely mad.'

'Yes,' agreed Russell. 'But to him it was logical. He was just trying to show the army they'd made a mistake. Serial killers often think they're behaving logically.'

'But logically in a crazy way,' said Scott.

'Yes,' replied Russell.

'And this is what? Your third or fourth serial killer?' asked Neville.

'Third,' replied Russell. She drank a little of her wine. 'All three very different in some ways, but very similar in others.'

'How do you mean?' asked Scott.

'Well, the first,' began Russell, 'was a woman, a nurse actually, who killed some of the old people she visited at home. In her mind they were too old to look after themselves and so they shouldn't be allowed to live.'

Russell drank some more wine.

'The second,' she continued, 'was a man whose girlfriend left him about five years before. Since then he'd had great difficulty in his relationships with women. The problem built up and up, and eventually he started killing young women in their twenties with blonde hair. Girls who reminded him of his ex-girlfriend.'

'And now a guy who wants to show the army that he knows how to kill, so that they'll let him join up,' added Scott.

'Exactly,' replied Russell.

'And how are they similar?' asked Neville.

'They show just how little it can take to turn the balance of the human mind upside down,' answered Russell. 'A failed attempt to join the army, breaking up with a girlfriend, being in a job where you end up hating the people you're supposed to be helping – these are things that people often experience at some time in their lives—'

'But it doesn't usually turn them into killers,' interrupted Scott.

'No, it doesn't,' said Russell. 'Normal people manage. They move on. They get a different job; they get a new girlfriend. But for a very few people it changes the balance of their minds just enough. They develop a strange, kind of poisonous, murdering logic that drives them to kill. And, having killed once ...'

Russell stopped speaking and looked down into her glass.

Scott put her hand on Russell's arm.

'It's over now, Fiona,' she said.

Russell looked up.

'Yes, it is,' she agreed. 'Until the next time.'